T0196348

SOVEREIGNTY
AND
BORDERS

SOVEREIGNTY

AND

BORDERS

EDGER J. BURTON

iUniverse

SOVEREIGNTY AND BORDERS
You Can't Have One without the Other

iUniverse books may be ordered through booksellers or by contacting:

iUniverse
1663 Liberty Drive
Bloomington, IN 47403
www.iuniverse.com
1-800-Authors (1-800-288-4677)

ISBN: 978-1-4917-8815-8 (sc)
ISBN: 978-1-4917-8814-1 (e)

Library of Congress Control Number: 2016901319

Print information available on the last page.

iUniverse rev. date: 01/21/2016

A truth: and there is no other truth, a nation without protected borders is not a nation at all; but an open invitation to chaos, to criminals, to subversives, to eventual oblivion and destined to become a mere foot note in the annals of history.

Such is the plight of those who today call "The United States of America" their homeland, their country, and many of the victims seem unaware of how it is being done, as well as in many cases that it is being done.

Although there are some Americans who are waking up and seeing the changes that are taking place on a national and international scale, as well as in their own communities, they are for the most part frustrated by the feeling of being helpless to stop the direction the country is heading.

However, there is still time to correct the situation by rejecting the current duplicitous politicians and their political parties that have for all intents and purposes surrendered not only our prosperity and our sovereignty, but our children's futures as well.

Our freedoms and our prosperity have apparently become expendable for their own perceived gain, or their own chosen ideology that runs counter to the "Constitutional Republic System" that our forefathers created.

Many Americans realize that the problem is an out of control, a bought and paid for political class that has literally betrayed them and are turning their country into a third world existence for future Americans; their children.

The United States is today being "fundamentally transformed" from a "Sovereign Constitutional Republic" into an international sanctuary for all who violate its borders with impunity, up to and including criminal aliens as well as the very real possibility of terrorists.

"The Constitutional Republic" given to us by our founders has over the years been in the process of a slow change; a change where our constitution and its guarantees are no longer honored as the law of the land.

Slowly over time, our "Founder's Constitutional Contract" created and ratified by the states and their people "the American People", has been replaced by the whims of an elite ruling class in a two party system and their donors, their financiers, their money masters.

The current situation today is that all prosperity, all of the Nations sovereignty, all freedoms are being erased by those who would turn "The United States of America" into their own plantation for personal gain with American citizens as their servants, and it is now being fast tracked.

So now we know what the campaign statement, "We are five days away from fundamentally transforming the United States of America" really meant, although not what many thought it meant.

The fundamental transformation referred to on the campaign trail wasn't described in any particular detail, so it was left up to each individual to draw their own conclusions as to what it meant.

How many people could have guessed that it meant an abandonment of long established principals; long established laws, long established international relationships with allies?

How many would have guessed that it meant a policy of open borders, sanctuary for those who enter the country illegally, protection for the criminal element among those that would enter the country illegally?

How many could have guessed that it meant a policy of furthering racial divisions, therefore erasing the progress accomplished over many years, over many generations of Americans?

As the truism says "a house, a nation divided will not stand" and the divisions are well under way, officially sanctioned by those who by the available evidence are instigating divisions by policies to divide by race, by age, by gender and ideology, in service to themselves and their own agenda, not to the American people.

How many Americans would have guessed that it meant that those who are charged with keeping our neighborhoods safe from criminals would come under official government attack to the point of being afraid to do their jobs resulting in a rise in crime across the board?

How many could have guessed that it meant that as a result, crime rates would spike and law enforcement officers would become the targets of an emboldened criminal element, and be killed because they were in their uniforms.

Obviously when dealing with people, there will inevitably be the occasional bad apple so to speak; however, the alternative would be a benefit for the criminals among us and current events are rapidly progressing in that direction.

If the above isn't an accurate description of the current situation where law enforcement agencies around the country are being effectively put on notice to proceed with caution, do your job and risk your own prosecution, or even worse being murdered, how else would anyone define it?

A government that was concerned about public safety, security, and the economic wellbeing of its citizens, would surely zero in on the real problems at hand.

Illegal immigration is especially demeaning economically on "African American" communities due to the war on Black Americans by the illegal aliens.

This Los Angeles Times article would be a good place to begin researching the basis for the above statement. HTTP://.latimes.com/la-op-hutchinson25nov25-story.html

What if many crime problems and many social problems could be solved by the alleviation of poverty in lower income communities?

Can they be? Of course they can, by allowing these communities to secure the employment opportunities available for their people, both young and old alike.

Earning a paycheck instead of having to depend on public assistance or illegal activity, would be a definite elevating experience for the individual as well as the community as a whole.

Employment opportunities opening up for American citizens trapped in poverty, demeaned communities will be a major step forward, they will become more prosperous as opportunities raise the prospects for a better life.

The new reality of many of today's social ills should begin correcting themselves as living standards increase and community leaders begin forming alliances to root out and eliminate drug dealers and street gangs for a better life for their children.

Beginning the experience of the individual advancing their skills and working their way up in life, should and more than likely would raise the self esteem of many, thereby raising the entire community.

However, today far too many of the available employment opportunities are going to illegal immigrants who then send a major portion of the money home, while these neighborhoods become stagnant, this resource, this money should be staying in and benefiting American citizens and their communities.

For any national government to fail to protect their borders while concentrating on policies that ignore their public safety obligations and demean the employment opportunities for their own people is insane to say the least.

How many Americans would have guessed that "hope and change" and "fundamental transformation" meant that our borders would become open doors to the world?

How many Americans would have guessed that once deported individuals would reenter our country multiple times knowing that there will be no real consequence for their actions or enforcement of our laws?

Now that the current administrations policies are plainly evident that federal immigration laws are in their view irrelevant and not to be effectively enforced the meaning of the campaigns "hope and change" and "fundamental transformation" should be plain to all.

My guess is that many of those who cheered the statement would not have done so if they had known that it meant competition for jobs from illegal aliens, while citizens and legal immigrants were unemployed.

Or, that it meant that aid intended for U.S. citizens would be going to illegal immigrants at taxpayer expense, far beyond our financial capabilities to sustain.

And, for sanctuary for all foreigners, even those who commit the most heinous of crimes against American citizens on American soil.

Slick professionally promulgated political slogans like "hope and change" and "fundamental transformation", are designed to allow those who hear them to draw their own opinions as to there meaning.

While the real meaning of campaign slogans, the politicians use to get elected may be and often are far different than the one people will believe them to be at the time.

Those who would gain by erasing America's borders beginning with the southern border are the advocates of one world government; a statement often described as a conspiracy theory.

However: if that isn't the goal being pursued by this administration as well as others before them as evidenced by the progression of movement, in that direction the result will eventually be the same; sovereignty lost.

To anyone who can see through the outright obfuscation and dogma that surrounds the subject, it is plain that intentional or not a one world government is on a fast track today.

When the government of a nation becomes an outlaw ignoring long established laws that were set in place to protect its sovereignty and its citizenry, ignoring its borders, that government and its politicians are in gross dereliction of their responsibilities to their people.

How else could a "National Government" that allows unchecked, unregulated illegal immigrant entry that is contrary to its laws across its borders without taking any affective action necessary to correct the situation be defined?

Many Americans today are aware of and opposed to sanctuary cities and counties, but fail to realize that The United States under the current administration's policies is in reality being "fundamentally transformed" into a sanctuary country.

Past administrations have done little or nothing either that would affect an improvement in the situation or the current border problems have been building up over many years, over many administrations on both sides of the political isle.

And what is the situation that would be described as untenable by many citizens today when it comes to America's borders?

All one has to do to get the answer is listen to news broadcasts that are telling us about the dangers that exists with the facts; facts about

American citizens that are being raped, robbed and murdered by people who shouldn't be in the country.

Americans are having their children targeted by the minions of foreign drug lords with criminal records who shouldn't be in the country.

Foreigners; the enforcers for the international drug trade, human smugglers and other various crimes are in many cases people who should not even be in the country, and obviously sanctuary cities and counties are guilty of violating law by aiding and abetting them.

Laws meant to protect the public safety, are being ignored by these purveyors of unlawful sanctuary policies that endanger their own citizens.

The only way to define the current situation is that like it or not, the United States is now under "de-facto transitional policies" to turn America into a sanctuary country for foreigners and the criminals among them.

There are millions of foreigners in the country today, some are here even though they have been deported multiple times and have returned multiple times knowing that they are protected by this administration's national sanctuary policies.

And this includes many with criminal felony records, guilty of extremely violent crimes that were committed right here on American soil against American citizens, as well as legal immigrants.

This doesn't take into account the fact that terrorists can enter the country without detection, along with the very real possibility that terrorist's along with their chosen weaponry are free to enter the country, and may already be here and by the evidence today, some definitely are here and active.

Not only standard military weapons, but up to and including the very real possibility of weapons of mass destruction could also be entering the country and could already be here, let us pray they are not.

Anyone who doesn't believe that this is a real and present danger, is not thinking rationally about the current turmoil, the violent hate America groups that exist around the world today; as well as the many that exist and are based right here in America.

Many would agree with the statement that American's have enough problems with crime and terrorist activity by those legally here without adding to the problem by allowing criminal aliens that enter the country through borders that are very literally open to them to become a factor.

To all that doubt that our out of control southern border isn't being taken advantage of by terrorists should do some research and discover the real story; the facts.

The following is excerpted from a declassified Department of Public Safety report prepared for Gov Greg Abbott of Texas, titled "Border Surge Report."

"Illegal Aliens from countries documented by the U.S. Department of State as having a known terrorism presence continue to be smuggled into Texas and throughout the nation on a regular basis, and it is impossible to determine how many of these individuals have actually entered the U.S. undected. Texas leads the nation in the aprehension of "special interest aliens" (SIA) and there is a legitimate concern that terriorists from around the world could expliot our countries porous southwest border to enter the U.S. undected, if they have not done so already."

How long will it take before America and its citizens become irrelevant in world affairs and even their own affairs at home if the government continues following the national sanctuary policies apparently in force at present?

The answer is already available, national sovereignty is already rapidly disappearing and being taken over by the U.N. as evidenced by U.S. treaty laws being subverted and ignored by the current administration's actions of taking purposed treaties to the U.N. before going to Congress.

In a recent action our own congress voted to change the rules for a particularly bad treaty that was overwhelmingly opposed by the American people allowing that two thirds was required to block.

The rules were reversed, under the previous rules a two thirds majority would be needed to pass it, so in reality it passed with some duplicitous legislator's help.

Another indicator of where our sovereignty is going away would be the new term for our economy; we no longer have an American economy, a free economy; it is now known as an arm of the world economy which is a highly controlled economy.

A glaring example of a nation in full "fundamental transformation" and the surrender of its sovereignty would be the present situation that is now seemingly in full government implementation on both the U.S. southern border as well as in the international arena.

The amount of historical fallacies and falsehoods surrounding the history of the American Southwest today is staggering, one could correctly use the term twisted history.

In the Beginning the new settlers from the U.S. were loyal to Mexico; many of the big names that are associated with the secession movement and the Texas rebellion today were indeed loyal to the Mexican government in the beginning.

The trouble began when Santa Anna took over the Mexican government by a coup and declared himself ruler for life and arbitrarily nullified the "Mexican Constitution."

Ponder this, one lays claim to a vast region of land; the region is already populated by others who have made it their home for thousands of years, for many thousands of generations.

When the claim by decree fails to come to fruition due to the lack of control and/or interest by ones own people, and others are invited into the territory who in time rebel as the region is taken over by a dictator; was it ever really your territory?

Although Mexico at one time claimed what is today the American Southwest any study of the time will reveal that they never had any real control of the region.

The area was controlled by the Apache, Comanche and other Native Indians who were indigenous to the region at the time.

Therefore the Mexican claim was a false and spurious claim then and so still is today, at best.

Today's claim that the Americans stole the territory from Mexico is equally as ridiculous.

How long did Mexico City have even a semblance of control over the region known today as the American Southwest?

The answer is "for only about twenty five years" during which time it was in reality under the affective control of the indigenous native populations who lived there.

Mexico City had no effective control; only by a decree that was unenforceable, and even that for all intents and purposes was slipping away until the Americans became a part of the equation.

Since Mexico wasn't in control at any time, the real control of the region was by the Indian tribes living there, Mexico City was desperate to find a way to take control of the region.

Mexicans at the time didn't want to live in today's American Southwest region so the government in Mexico City turned to the Americans for help.

Since the Government in Mexico City could not protect its people who might go to the area the plan to encourage Americans who were brave enough to settle the region and swear allegiance to Mexico was set in place.

In the 1820s the government in Mexico City began giving land to Americans who were willing to settle there in an effort to gain at least some control to legitimize their claim.

For a short period of time the arrangement seemed to be going well until the Mexican Government was overthrown in a military coup by the self appointed Dictator Santa Anna and his nullification of the "Mexican Constitution" by decree.

The overthrow of the Mexican Government by Santa Anna was the beginning of the end for the allegiance to Mexico of the new settlers from America that eventually led to the beginning of the Texas rebellion.

Assertions of historical rights and claims by Mexicans over present day U.S. territory are mainly based on assumptions that they have preemptive special rights in the American Southwest, assertions that are patently untrue since it is based on falsehoods.

How can one reasonably claim something that was never under their control as evidenced by the fact that they encouraged Americans to settle the region since their own citizens would not?

How could a claim to ownership of territory by Mexico be valid when it was still under the effective control of an indigenous people who had lived there for millennia?

I guess the real question today is; how can any Mexican of today make the statement "the United states stole the American Southwest from Mexico" without any thought processes kicking in before making that statement?

By their standards, built into the claim, how can it, or could it, be stolen from Mexico if, by the same reasoning they attempted but without success to steal it from the indigenous Indians who were already there?

Very literally what they are saying is, "forget the fact that we tried to steal it by decree from the Indigenous people who lived there," but failed while we make this statement.

The Mexican claim to the American Southwest was eventually challenged by people who had entered the region by invitation and began settlements, ranches, farms, etc, and were disenchanted to say the least by the takeover by a dictator of the government in Mexico City.

The overthrow of the Mexican Government by Santa Anna who declared himself ruler for life with the power to rule by fiat and nullify the Mexican Constitution that the new arrivals from America were given the contractual right to live under was the beginning catalyst for the Texas rebellion.

Mexico's Constitution was based on "a Federal Government of Sovereign States" as the U.S. Constitution was; it was a constitution that gave considerable rights to the individual Mexican states.

Adding insult to injury in 1830, the Mexican congress passed a law saying that no more Americans could immigrate to Texas and it also allowed for the garrisoning of convict troops to police the area.

Living under the adverse conditions of being under the rule of a Dictator while being policed by convicts in military uniform was unacceptable to the Texans and that fact only intensified the conditions for the eventual rebellion.

Refusing to live under the betrayal of a despot dictator the inhabitants of the territory who found themselves under an untenable situation soon made the choice, live under a dictatorship, or throw off the dictator's yoke and eventually join a constitutionally limited federal government with states rights that was still available to them.

So in point of fact the rebellion by Texans was started by the Dictator Santa Anna's actions.

Apparently the crude mentality of the Dictator Santa Anna wasn't capable of rational thought.

By the historical evidence, devoid of any sign of logic or reasoning Santa Anna began a campaign of despotic determination based on a slash and burn and kill rampage to establish himself by example as the all powerful master over the region.

A reasonably intelligent person should have foreseen that the unrest due to their actions could result in exactly the course that history records.

Instead of a thought out response to the growing unrest in Texas Santa Anna chose chaos and carried out a bloody razed earth campaign evidenced by history to hold on to his assumed, self appointed, dictatorial rule over the region.

He began his campaign by moving ten thousand Mexican troops into the region and attacking the Alamo and ordering the death of everyone inside.

The apparent intent of instilling fear into the Texans was the goal, but in reality the affect was just the opposite, the resentment and the anger that resulted due to this action at the Alamo only increased the resolve of the Texans.

In the end Santa Anna was defeated and the region eventually became a part of The United Sates of America but today the Mexicans as well as others come into the United States and act as if they somehow have a prior right, a prior claim to the area.

Although rejected and defeated by people who were living under the despotism of a tyrannical dictator at the time the Mexican government today acts as if the American Southwest is still a part of their domain.

There are many Hispanic Americans whose families have been proud Americans for generations that resent the influx of illegals who are here; not only Hispanic, but from all over the world.

Mexicans as well as many others ignore the border between the two countries under the spurious and false supposition that they somehow have the historical right to do so.

In many cases they bring with them the culture of crime, corruption and disrespect for laws that they are trying to escape from, and by the available evidence they are seemingly blind to that fact as they endeavor to remake America in Mexico's image.

If they are trying to free themselves from an unbearable situation why escape to the United States and then apparently endeavor to turn their new existence into a mirror image of the country that they have risked all to flee from?

During the early years of the United States native peoples in the region resisted the newcomers; as a result a period known in U.S. history as the Indian wars ensued and ended in treaties with the differing Native American indigenous tribes.

Yes, the wars were bloody and heinous atrocities on both sides were committed; however, in the end agreements were reached, agreements between the U.S. government and the various tribes' leaders that are still the law of the land today.

By way of these agreements between the Native American populations living in the U.S. today and the U.S. government; the U. S. government has a measure of legitimacy in that area, and in many instances still gives them opportunities for a redress of complaints.

However, no such agreements with the indigenous peoples living in what is today the American southwest were ever made or sought by the Mexican government of the time.

Throughout human history wars and there accompanying inhumanity towards one's fellow man have flourished, driven in many instances by the coveting of one nation for the territory of a neighboring country.

Wars instigated by religiously oriented warlords who had/have the goal of subjugating others and ruling by force; dominating all others who are of a differing faith have and still do commit heinous acts of cold blooded murder as a means to an end.

Both these past and present would be overlords are the destroyers of lives, destroyers of entire civilizations while claiming the right to do so in the name of their God.

The history books are replete with examples of genocide, suffering, degradation and atrocities that have taken place in the pursuit of empire by nations and religions whose leaders were hungry for power and territory with dreams of world domination.

Beginning with territorial rights claims over a region of a neighboring country has often been a common theme for those seeking to create or expand an Empire.

As pointed out above Mexico City had no effective control and even that for all intents and purposes was slipping away until the Americans became a part of the equation.

Mexico's government could not get its citizens to move to its northern frontier since they could not be protected, a fact that was the reason why in the 1820s it began giving land to Americans who were willing to settle there under a "Constitutional Contract" and become loyal to the "Mexican Constitutional Government" that Santa Anna ended by a coup.

"The Constitutional Contract" was broken and therefore ended by Santa Anna not the Texans who came to the area in good faith and found themselves betrayed.

Assertions of historical claims by Mexicans over present day U.S. territory are mainly based on assumptions that they have preemptive special rights in the American Southwest and these assertions are patently untrue since it is based on falsehoods that a little research will easily disprove.

Conflict is a guaranteed result when people in one country begin making claims and asserting proprietary rights claims to territory of another neighboring country.

For every action there is a reaction, the actions by Santa Anna and his supporters were what led to the reaction of the Texans; the Texas rebellion.

In general the Mexican Constitution of the time gave considerable rights to the individual Mexican states; it was based on "a federal government of sovereign states" as the U.S. constitution was.

Over time as history repeats itself Americans now find themselves today heading down the same dubious road as the Texans with their original constitutional rights being eroded and lawful protections required by their constitution ignored by their federal government.

The Actions by the Mexican Congress in the 1830s, of the passing of a law saying that no more Americans could immigrate to Texas along with the added insult of the garrisoning of convict troops to police the area was another one of a growing number of deciding factors involved.

As the dictator's injustices multiplied, compounded over time, history shows that the Texans decision was rebellion against tyranny.

Justifiably refusing to live under the betrayal of a despot dictator the inhabitants of the territory who found themselves living under an unacceptable situation soon made a choice, live under a dictatorship, or throw off the dictator's yoke and eventually join a constitutionally limited government that was still available to them at the time.

By the historical evidence available Santa Anna began his campaign of subjugating the Texans with an indisputable inhuman act at the Alamo when he ordered the execution of everyone inside.

Apparently with his crude mentality Santa Anna wasn't capable of rational thought as he attempted to set an example with a military campaign to end the Texan's rebellion; he attacked the Alamo giving the order to kill everyone inside including the wounded that were no longer a threat.

After the Alamo Santa Anna continued to pursue the carrying out of his bloody razed earth campaign against the Texans as evidenced by history to hold on to his assumed, self appointed, dictatorial rule over the region.

This was a mistake on his part "Remember the Alamo" became the battle cry of Texans who were even more determined to take themselves out from under his despotic rule.

In the end the Texans rebellion was successful and Santa Anna was defeated and the region eventually became a part of The United Sates of America.

However, today the Mexicans as well as others from all over the world come into the United States across the Mexican/American Border and act as if they somehow have a right to do so based on a prior claim to the area.

Although rejected and defeated by people who were living under the despotism of a tyrannical dictator at the time the Mexican Government today acts as if the American Southwest is somehow still a part of their domain.

Americans have every reason to wonder if their federal government isn't under de-facto agreement with Mexico on the issue as they refuse to take control and defend the border with Mexico and protect American citizens.

Mexico by their actions ignores the border between the two countries as if it didn't exist under the apparent although spurious and false reasoning that historically they somehow have the right to do so.

The following is from an article in the Washington Times: "Armed Mexican troops and police regularly stray across the U.S. border, according to statistics from the "Department of Homeland Security" provided to Congress on Tuesday that indicate more than 500 of them have jumped the border in the past decade."

Also from the Washington Times: "An Arizona congressman yesterday demanded the State Department take "immediate diplomatic action" to stop Mexican military incursions into the United States, saying the U.S. Border Patrol Agents face a continuing threat of being killed by rogue soldiers protecting drug smugglers."

However; the U.S. Government continues to allow the border incursions and the accompanying harm to its citizens and legal immigrants, and the potential for harm to its Border Patrol Agents.

It hasn't been that long ago that a U.S. Border Patrol Agent was killed in just such a situation, murdered by drug smugglers protecting their cross border contraband.

The military weapon used in the murder of the American Border Patrol Agent by the drug cartel's smugglers was one of many weapons recently sanctioned by the U.S. government for sale across the Mexican border.

There is evidence that suggests that the sale of the weapons in question were not only sanctioned for sale across the Mexican Border, but the transactions were encouraged by some U.S. government officials under the code name "Fast and Furious."

The violence that is spreading throughout the nation due to present border policies is only being minimally challenged by the U.S. government, and often by lip service and little else.

As American politicians have postured, debated and argued on the subject of border security for many years and the debate is still going on today, and nothing has been done by either party to improve the situation.

It's as if the subject as a debate is more important to them to use as a tool while pandering for donations and votes than addressing the problem and securing the border to protect America's sovereignty and its citizen.

One could rightfully describe the situation as our political parties holding the nations security and the safety of American citizen's hostage for political gain.

Instead of addressing the situation with serious intent, with action, one party in particular is apparently using our borders to advance their agenda of passing legislation to retroactively reward past unlawful acts by legalizing illegal aliens after the fact.

The objections by the other party to doing so are for the most part a subject to be avoided by them with the exception of a few who make the occasional statement against this form of amnesty and then continue to do nothing of substance to prevent it.

The safety and security of American citizens and legal immigrants are not the focus of any politician who demands that those who have broken our laws be rewarded.

Our Constitution plainly says no "Ex-Post-Facto Laws," meaning that no law may be passed that would countermand a previous law and be applied retroactively.

A law can be repealed and replaced by legislation but not ignored while still on the books as law.

Or simply put a future law set in place can not constitutionally apply to the past as in someone who was convicted of selling Marijuana illegally could not have that crime become legal retroactively if the sale of Marijuana became legal in the future and be released from the past penalties for their actions.

When unlawful behavior is made irrelevant contrary to law after the fact by those who make the laws they themselves have become outlaws by their actions, and any other interpretation of this fact are both spurious and dubious at best.

In many cases the illegal immigrants bring with them the culture of crime, corruption and disrespect for laws that they are trying to escape from, and by the available evidence they are seemingly blind to that fact as they endeavor to remake America into the image of the country they have escaped from.

Many immigrants both legal and illegal come to The U.S. with the attitude that by being determined to do so they will eventually change our laws to suit themselves by instituting their own religious laws that favor them to replace our equality under the law system regardless of religion.

I have heard the suggestion made that at the time of swearing in new immigrant citizens a part of the procedure should be the following mandatory yes affirmation of the following question.

"As part of your citizenship oath, will you live under and be faithful to American law; will you support the U.S. freedom of religion laws regardless of faith and reject any countermanding religious law system?"

There are also immigrants both legal and illegal that are here and are trying to change our immigration laws to literally open the proverbial flood gates and overwhelm our country and its citizens.

Again I ask; if they are trying to free themselves from the earlier described situation why escape to the United States and then apparently endeavor to turn their new existence into a mirror image of the country they have risked all to flee from?

There are many differing chosen methods of empire building in world history. They range from the obvious, by way of force, conquering armies, financial domination and Religion to name a few.

A current example taking place today would be the Russian method of taking a neighbor's territory as in their annexation of the Crimea region of the Ukraine.

The dubious excuse for doing so was the fact that many of those who had immigrated to the area were of Russian descent, and so the territory was now by default Russian.

However, the real reason for Russia's takeover of the Ukrainian Crimea region was the acquisition of a militarily significant port resource.

Now Russia has moved on to supporting efforts by ethnic Russians living in other parts of the Ukraine to secede from the Ukraine.

The next logical step following historical patterns would be that Russia eventually would make the effort to annex any former Ukrainian territory if the secession effort is successful.

The driving forces behind each attempt at empire building or expansion of an existing empire whether successful or a failure has always been and always will be the expansion of power over people and the acquisition of territory and access to their valuable natural resources.

The present day would be empire builders both secular and religious, the would-be rulers of as many people and territory and the increased wealth involved are every bit as determined as their counterparts were throughout human history.

A method of governing has been introduced in recent history and has been employed with great success, establishing Constitutional

Republics with limited federal governments and a free enterprise economic system where all may participate with inalienable rights guaranteed by a "Constitutional Contract" to all citizens.

The above described system of governance was set in place establishing The United States of America creating by far the most successful nation in existence today.

If not for the destruction of the "Constitutional Mexican Government" of the time by the Dictator Santa Anna the history of the Americas today would be far different.

The United States today might well have prosperous neighbors on both borders that respect the territories of the other as the Canadians and Americans do.

However, today our founding contract accepted by ratification by the states, The Constitution of The United States is in many instances being ignored today by our politicians.

The rights set forth in the U.S. founding document at the new nations beginning The Constitution of The United States established a limited form of federal government restricting federal powers over the states and their people.

A "Bill of Rights" was established identifying in detail the new national government's powers and duties and in great detail spelling out the powers forbidden to it and reserved to the states and their people.

Now let us turn our attention to the national defense responsibilities of the Federal Government which are "We the People of The United States, in Order to form a more perfect union, establish justice, insure domestic tranquility, and provide for the common defense ..."

The very beginning of our founding document plainly lays the responsibility for the defense of the states and a peaceful society on the new federal government.

So why do we literally have a foreign invasion through our Southern Border States and crimes being committed by illegal immigrants and foreign criminal organizations against American citizens and politicians in all parts of the country and the federal government get by with ignoring it?

Why do we have foreigners coming from all over the world on visas, student visas, and tourist visas and then staying without consequence?

It has recently come to the attention of the American people that these people are not being properly vetted and as a result despicable crimes are therefore being committed against American citizens on American soil.

Our federal government at present not only ignores these obvious very serious problems for the states and their people, especially the Border States, it also challenges any state that attempts to protect themselves from this invasion and sides with the illegal invaders.

When a political party, or a politician, or the courts come down on the side of preventing the logical government's responsibility of ensuring that our security and rights as citizens are a first priority something is bad wrong.

Any government that was living up to its responsibilities to its people would enforce the laws, our border security, our sovereignty and our rights under our constitutional contract.

The immensely successful United States of America, a Constitutional Republic with elected officials shares a common border with Mexico that is being violated on a daily basis.

Mexico is a country where domestic crime and poverty are rampant and international crime in the form of drug dealing and money laundering, smuggling, kidnapping and human trafficking with the apparent collusion of some in our own government is a common factor.

The United States is a country where the average citizen's standard of living is good, at least so far, where opportunities are there for those who are willing and driven to success can achieve their goals.

Mexico however is a country where crime with government collusion in many cases; and poverty with government indifference are the rule, not the exception.

The United States is a country that people from all over the world want to immigrate to.

In stark contrast Mexico is a country where its citizens in many cases risk great hardship to escape from.

Mexicans pay huge sums to human smugglers to take them across the Mexican American Border into the United States in the hope of escaping to a better way of life that they are aware exists just across that border.

The problem for the American citizen is that along with those seeking a better way of life the border smugglers also double as drug smugglers; and human traffickers for illicit purposes.

The following are excerpts from a United States Border Patrol website article.

"The Mexican sex slave trafficking cartel is called "Los Lenones," and is composed of nearly 20 major trafficking groups and more than 100 smaller groups."

"This is a real industry and "Los Lenones" even takes orders, and fills them as needed to service the slave-filled brothels of America."

"Commercial airplanes arrive at Mexico City's airport every day carrying groups of these girls."

"The Mexican officials are in collusion with the traffickers and these girls are separated from the passenger flow and quickly shunted out to waiting cars."

The shame and disgrace here is not Mexico's alone, but equally shared by Americans, their politicians and the U.S. government that allows this to continue happening and our own governments' failure to address the criminal activity taking place by eliminating the open border sex slave trade routs.

These girls are daughters, granddaughters and someone's child that are being destroyed and having the hope of a normal happy life ended by criminals both inside and outside of government in Mexico, and by U.S. government inaction.

If this human tragedy was brought to the attention of American citizens by way of a media that reported these facts with a mass campaign that made them aware could this extremely evil and outrageous practice be ended?

Those on this side of the border who are a part of the border sex slave trade should be ferreted out and given life sentences, stripped of all property and even that would be far less than they deserve.

In a truly just and fair system of justice, once investigated and convicted these domestic sex slavers and their cross border counterparts should be imprisoned for life and all their properties, monies and any and all illicit gains awarded to the victims of the trade.

Americans fought a civil war to end the heinous practice of human slavery that in many cases included sex slavery, so the answer should be plain to all.

Many would surely think of their daughters and granddaughters and not only get involved, but become committed activists and demand that our government make it a priority to end the southern border sex slave trade once and for all by closing down the slavers open border routs into the U.S.

At best the currently existing inhumane situation for these girls could be described as a disgraceful cross border criminal enterprise that has a shared blame with our own government and the American people for allowing an open border that aids and abets the cross border sex slave trade trafficking criminals, both Mexican and American.

Again, the following are excerpted and taken from the U.S. Border Patrol website.

"The flood of Mexican illegal aliens across the United States southern border is wanton, violent, continuous, and unchecked.

That is the truth; there is no "alternate" truth."

"While much of the US / Mexico border is a dangerous place during the day, it becomes a place of great violence at night. Most illegal aliens cross the border at night. Most of the ranch burglaries, assaults, and murders are perpetrated along the border at night."

"Along the U.S. border with Mexico there are 43 Ports of Entry. Of these 43 entry points, 18 are in Texas. Nearly all of these Ports of Entry are connected to major highway systems in Texas."

"The illegal alien smugglers, drug smugglers and criminal gangs use these major highways to then spread into America."

"These gangs -- including MS 13 -- act as the "army" for the Mexican drug cartels and enforce their will here in the United States."

"The border violence against American citizens inside the United States has never been as high as it is today.

Further, the threat is not just the gangs from Mexico, Honduras, Guatemala, and El Salvador."

"The threat is also from Middle Eastern individuals being moved from Central America through Mexico, into Texas, and into the rest of United States."

So, do you realize that we have an extremely serious border problem; the U.S. border patrol says that we do?

Does anyone doubt that if the situation continues unabated being overwhelmed to the point of no return is fast approaching on the horizon throughout the country, as well as right here in our own communities?

And it isn't just Mexico; the following articles posted below are from the LA TIMES;

"Three young men were killed and a fourth wounded in what police suspect was an attack by the notorious MS-13 street gang. Police were searching for five or six assailants."

"Witness said that before shooting, the gunmen shouted "Mara Salvatrucha," the formal name of the Salvadoran gang that traces its origins to Los Angeles in the 1980s."

"Officials say 19 of those arrested had warrants for murder and an additional 15 for rape or sexual assault."

"One man in L.A. was arrested on suspicion of narcotics trafficking after law enforcement officials said they found he was allegedly selling methamphetamine within 100 yards of a school."

Now, is it only those living in the border areas that are being demeaned, and their children being targeted and exploited by these south of the border drug cartels?

Not according to the above quoted articles from the LA Times, although the border areas are more exposed to the problem it is nationwide.

And now to go directly to the heart of the problem, and it isn't only Mexico or the other South American countries involved.

The problem is our own political parties, both Democrat and Republican who continue to pass the buck so to speak while some actually stonewall the issue for their own reasons.

The Democrats reasons are for support and money from pro-illegals and some Republicans although not as blatant or as many for support and money from pro-business factions wanting cheap labor.

The Democrats believe that an open border will eventually lead to more illegal immigrants from the south being given amnesty and in time being given citizenship.

Their long term goal simply put is "votes illegal or not" that will increase there power base and likewise sustain them in power and allow them to further the goal of even more socialism being set into place here in our country.

The questions that come to mind are; what are they protecting, are they protecting their own agenda of using our southern border to gain a dominant position, do they believe they can't win a fair election and achieve their chosen agendas with only those authorized to do so voting?

Even though we are already over extended in our financial capabilities; and the result will obviously lead to eventual inevitable bankruptcy for the nation they welcome the cross border illegal immigration as a means to an end.

Our system of political donations depends on reciprocal actions from politicians who take the donations knowing that a quid-pro-quo will be required for future support, for even more campaign contributions in the future.

Many politicians on both sides of the isle have a reason to pander for money from the business interests that gain from cheap labor; cheap labor that benefits the donor by keeping wages low.

Another part of the problem is labor unions wanting to expand their membership and their incomes that are financially supporting politicians who will take their money and oppose any affective border security policy.

If the current situation continues the nation's financial situation will worsen, not being able to sustain the added expense of the inevitable government services for the illegal immigrants national bankruptcy will inevitably sooner or later be the result.

The above mentioned government services include educating the children of illegal immigrant's their medical expenses, the expense of incarceration for violations of law and public aid although many still deny it even though it is obvious.

The illegal immigrants who enter the country looking for work will work for less than an American citizen due to the often denied fact that many will upon arrival begin receiving social services such as welfare and food stamps shortly after arrival; therefore, those who use them are being subsidized by the American taxpayer.

"In 2012, 51 percent of households headed by an immigrant (legal or illegal) reported that they used at least one welfare program during the year, compared to 30 percent of native households. Welfare in this study includes Medicaid and cash, food, and housing programs ..." Center For Immigration Studies.

The labor unions know full well that the illegal immigrants who enter the country looking for work will work for less than an American citizen and keep wages for Americans; including their own members and legal immigrants depressed.

The above seems to be irrelevant to the major unions, gaining favor by supporting the illegal immigrants in the prospect of getting them to join and increase their income by way of union dues would be a good guess as to the why.

Anyone who denies that the illegal alien factor doesn't affect wages for American workers is either denying facts that they are aware of, or are themselves pandering for donations, or are benefiting from the cheap illegal labor, or want more socialism, or have a deficiency in their cognitive mental abilities.

As the saying goes "figures lie and liars figure" is alive and well in the pro-illegal immigrant groups on both sides of the political spectrum that make the claim that the illegal immigrants commit fewer crimes than American citizens do.

However: this is by the available evidence denying the truth and supporting the lie; in all reality their crimes are hugely disproportionate to their numbers as "The Bipartisan Sentencing Commission" reports.

According to "The Bipartisan Sentencing Commission" a report which plainly puts the lie to the denier's false claims and tells a far different story, the truth.

"The Bipartisan Sentencing Commission report supports that the number of illegal immigrants in this country who amount to 3.5% of the population, accounted for an astonishing 35.6% of federal sentences, although amnesty/open borders advocates have claimed for years that illegal immigrants commit far fewer crimes than citizens, but in reality their crimes are hugely disproportionate to their numbers" ... Lou Dobbs.

At this point consider this; the crime rate numbers for illegal aliens officially reported are in fact higher than the numbers reported due to the policies of sanctuary cities and counties not reporting on the amount of illegal alien crimes versus citizen crimes in their areas.

Due to the "don't ask, don't tell" policies of sanctuary cities and counties there is no way to accurately correlate the real numbers of illegal alien crimes.

A crime is committed in a sanctuary city or county by a criminal alien and the government never knows the crime was by an illegal, so obviously it is not counted as an illegal alien crime.

There are nearly three hundred officially declared sanctuary cities and counties in the U.S. a fact that can be confirmed by a simple web research on the numbers.

There are many Americans who don't realize that sanctuary cities and counties even exist; however, they do and chances are that many people are living in one without their knowledge.

What is a sanctuary city or county, and what does this mean when it comes to public safety and security for Americans and legal immigrants?

This will undoubtedly sound incredulous to many Americans and legal immigrants, but it means that law enforcement is by sanctuary policies forbidden to inquire about ones legal status when that person has been arrested for any crime up to and including felonies.

Some local law enforcement agencies police/sheriffs welcome the policy as a benefit to them of less responsibility making their jobs easier, even though it means added danger for the people they are supposed to serve.

Obviously when law enforcement goes along with anyone who tells them to ignore a crime, any crime, and illegal immigration is a federal crime, and they do so for any reason they are not fit to hold that position.

Many have seen the news reports about the murder of a woman in San Francisco who was murdered by an criminal illegal alien immigrant with a record of numerous felonies and had been deported 9 times.

He told the police that he had come back to San Francisco because it was a sanctuary city, so he knew that by being there he would avoid another deportation.

On July 24 an illegal alien broke into the home of a Woman in her sixties, an Air Force Veteran in "Santa Maria, CA" he proceeded to sexually assault her and then beat her mercilessly with a hammer; she died later at the hospital from her wounds.

The local Police Chief rightfully called it a crime with a blood trail that reached from Washington DC to his City and into the Woman's home and for all intents and purposes he was right on.

The first above murder that took place in San Francisco made the news, and the other was reported by only one major news outlet until much later.

However, these are only two of the many such murders and other crimes committed by illegal immigrants that never make it to the public's attention thanks in many cases to a compliant pro-illegal news media.

For anyone who wants the truth; for the most part with the real numbers, a simple web search will probably shock you.

Adding insult to injury this is from "CBS news Los Angeles."

Huntington Park: "Huntington Park is making history and not everyone is happy about it."

"Councilman Jhonny Pineda announced at Monday night's city council meeting the appointment of two undocumented immigrants as Councilman."

If this isn't taking the extreme to beyond the pale nothing is; illegal aliens as a part of a local government in California?

However, many Americans could well be unaware that they themselves are living in a city or country with the same policy as San Francisco.

It doesn't take a lot of research to discover that California is actually a Sanctuary State, just look up "The Trust Act" that says that law enforcement must cooperate with immigration authorities and then goes on to make it nearly impossible if not impossible to do so is the state law.

It surprised me when watching a national news program I heard the news anchor mention that my city and county is a sanctuary city and county, so I began to do some research.

I soon discovered that he was right, and that two particularly gruesome murders, a woman who was beaten to death with a bat, and a man who was shot and his body was dumped in a wooded area and set on fire to destroy evidence that had recently been in the local news was committed by an illegal alien with a criminal record who had been deported multiple times but kept coming back to his/this sanctuary city.

I began talking to people about what I had found and the reaction was "Are you sure?"

After proving it to them their reaction was "Why didn't the local news report that the man was a criminal alien, and that he was still here even though he was deported many times, or that we live in a criminal alien sanctuary city and county?"

Good question right, however the better question is why people are putting up with a so-called news media that hides the facts from them and allow them to get away with it, after all isn't withholding information and reporting only selected parts of a story just another way of lying?

A formal sanctuary city or county is one with a written policy passed by a local government entity identifying it as a sanctuary for illegal immigrants, as such they are readily identifiable, but how many others that have sanctuary policies that are practiced but not written into their codes?

A city or county could well be practicing sanctuary policies even if they are not in writing, as such they would be much harder to identify, and without your knowledge you could be living in one of them.

In total disregard and violation of the "IIRIRA" the federal law that requires local governments to cooperate with federal authorities, ICE and DHS on the federal immigration laws these sanctuary cities and counties both shield their criminal activity as well as allow illegal aliens to benefit from taxpayer funded government services.

The real effect of Sanctuary cities and counties are two fold, as such they are literally protecting illegal aliens involved in criminal activities, drug dealers, gangs, rapists, terrorist cells, cross border human traffickers and therefore are guilty of aiding and abetting them in their crimes; a felony by law.

Second,: obviously by harboring the criminal element among those entering the country illegally along with others these criminal aliens are increasing the very real likely hood of legal residence falling victim to a protected class of criminals.

The Governor of Main by EO and Utah by Legislation have turned their entire states into illegal alien sanctuaries with Main giving them state driver's license which can get them American taxpayer funded benefits.

After a review of the facts and the available evidence how could anyone disagree with the statement that this country, contrary to established written law is a De-Facto illegal alien sanctuary country?

Why does a state governor get by with issuing an Executive Order that countermands i.e. flies in the face of established federal immigration laws?

Why does a state legislature get by with instituting a law that is blatantly contrary to federal immigration laws, an area of law that constitutionally does not belong to the states?

The state of Washington currently gives state driver's license to illegal aliens in that state that can get them taxpayer funded government services; so by their policies they are an apparent "De-Facto illegal alien sanctuary State."

How by any means possible could anyone honestly judge the current state, city, counties and federal government's policies and actions as anything other than illegal by established law?

How could anyone not be plainly aware in point of fact that a U.S. illegal alien sanctuary policy is definitely the policy in effect nationally as well as in some states and local communities?

Since they allow sanctuary cities and counties to go unchecked, unchallenged, the present federal government administration is by apparent design supporting illegal immigrants helping them evade federal immigration laws and stay in the country illegally.

Our politicians and our courts know full well that reentry after a deportation is a federal felony by law subject to prison, but by their inaction and collusion are for their own chosen duplicitous reasons share in the resulting crimes committed against American citizens and legal immigrants.

Any attempt to construe the situation otherwise is ludicrous and our politicians on both sides of the isle should and need to be called out on their failure to take the appropriate action by the American people.

Any agency from the city, county, state, or the federal government up to and including the "Federal Department of Justice" by refusing to take the actions required by law are guilty of criminal collusion to evade the law.

To sum up the situation Americans and legal immigrants have fallen victim to an out of control "Lawless Federal Government" too out of control lawless states, too outlaw county and city governments and Sheriff's departments.

The courts have protected illegal aliens at the expense of public safety as well as the right to have their tax dollars spent on those entitled to them, and not used to support illegal activity.

According to the Merriam Webster Dictionary a sanctuary is defined as where someone or something is protected or given shelter as in: the protection that is provided by a safe place a place of refuge and protection, the immunity from law attached to a sanctuary.

It is directly the fault of the United States federal government as well as state and local governments and particularly elected local Sheriffs when their citizens and legal immigrants fall victim to the crimes of robbery, theft, rape, burglary, assault and murder committed by people that are in the country illegally and protected under current policies.

The fact that this administration has turned the U.S. into a literal sanctuary nation for foreign criminals and subversives and past administrations have done little or nothing on the issue to enforce the existing laws and remedy the current untenable situation is unacceptable.

Why do our politicians act as if it would take some grandiose action on their part to remedy the situation the American people find themselves in when the answer is right there in front of them? (And us)

The problems on our southern border are compounded by a two fold factor, one would be the Mexican governments disrespect for international law; the other would be our own government at many levels disrespect for American laws and American citizens.

Why does the subject of border security always end up in a debate on whether or not a border wall/fence between the two countries is the only solution?

I would contend that a selectively placed border wall/fence would be a part of any long term effective border security, but only a part.

A border wall/fence would be expensive to build; expensive to maintain; expensive to guard since the wall/fence itself would have to be protected.

All one has to do to see just how effective border walls/fences are is to find and watch the many videos of illegal aliens scaling the few existing fences and scurrying off into the country.

At this point it would be non-productive to point out the problems without pointing out that there is a well thought out solution.

The solution to be truly effective and affordable to begin with already exists and is in place that would begin ending the border crises within a short period of time with a little effort to set it up.

Why not employ a system that is already here and ready to set in place that in the beginning would eliminate some of the need for expensive fences, walls, as well as the present and much of the future costs involved?

Cut off the temptation of jobs for those who would cross the border illegally and you have a definite beginning, then Americans and legal immigrants looking for work would be able to find jobs and better employment.

Many argue and appear to believe that there are far too many illegal immigrants in the country to deport; however, there is a method for correcting that situation by removing their incentive to stay.

By way of making E-Verify mandatory by law it is reasonable to believe that a correction in the current situation would begin immediately.

Over what should logically be a fairly short period of time the current border situation would begin to correct itself; then selectively add any fence or wall and manpower in places where the problems are more acute.

E-Verify the federal employment act should be made mandatory and that would begin ending the problem as it would require by law that potential employers confirm the immigration status of applicants within a matter of minutes, or even within seconds.

How hard would it be to put teeth into the law sufficient enough to ensure compliance?

How hard would it be to take the E-Verify system that exists and is working to the next step and add the necessary additions to the already existing; already working, already in place program?

Think about it; build a nearly two thousand mile long wall/fence in rough terrain, complete with guard towers, complete with roads to service the wall/fence, complete with facilities for the personnel to man it, eventually adding helicopter pads etc.

The logistics involved in building a two thousand mile long border wall/fence, maintaining and enforcing that border wall or fence would undoubtedly be a major problem in itself and could well be a cost prohibitive factor.

Since the problem has grown by leaps and bounds to the point of fast becoming an emergency so to speak, time is running out for something to be done.

However the virtual system proposed here would eliminate a whole host of problems; mainly the above logistics considerations involved, and would make the future venues for court challenges far more irrelevant.

The Courts including the Supreme Court would have to contort both themselves and the constitution to the point of twisting both the law as well as themselves into a pretzel.

Does anyone believe that any undertaking to build a border wall/fence will not be challenged in the courts ad-nauseum as the environmental groups along with any and everything the pro illegal groups can come up with?

The legal antics to stonewall the building of a border wall/fence would be horrendous, the environmental impact statements and the endangered species act are but two that immediately come to mind since they have already been brought up by pro illegal groups.

Make the choice to begin with a mandatory E-Verify system and then define where walls or fences that were strategically located in places that were still problem areas should be set in place.

A wall/fence that wouldn't need protecting physically; a cyber wall; a virtual wall that would extend well into the interior of the county would be far less expensive to put in place as a beginning, and would need very little future maintenance, and the beginnings of such a wall already exists.

Any challenges to this virtual wall should instantly be recognized by the American people for what it would truly be; a desperate attempt by open borders advocate groups and politicians to prevent any control of the border.

At this point one might wonder and begin asking why the cross border drug trade, the despicable cross border sex slave trade that beyond a doubt completely destroys the lives of the girls involved that our border patrol site tells us exists isn't widely known, isn't being reported by the news Medias.

Could it be that duplicitous politicians and a compliant news media know that if it became common knowledge that the outcry by the American people would force them to take control of our southern border?

Since the rape, robbery, assault and murders of American citizens currently in the news is making many Americans finally pay attention; how would they react to the knowledge that helpless girls are being bought and sold, enslaved, raped and some more than likely killed by open cross border criminal organizations?

As an in place mandatory law the Courts and Judges, even the Supreme Court would be hard pressed to try and invent ways to allow it to be circumvented; even those who by their present positions evidently would want to do so.

The beginning of any project starts with a plan; then is put into motion by laying the groundwork.

E-Verify is a widely accepted tool that already exists that is available to business as well as immigration enforcement, making accountability a part of hiring only people who are authorized for employment in the U.S. the responsibility of all involved.

"E-Verify is internet based and its most impressive features are its speed and accuracy, it is a free, fast, online service that verifies employee eligibility within as little as three to five seconds.".. ... Source USCIS.gov.

"E-Verify is used by 600.000 employers of all sizes, one of the federal government's highest rated services for customer satisfaction." ... Source USCIS.gov.

According to the U.S. Census Bureau data only about 3% of all U.S. employers use the system, and that needs to change now; by law.

Why not make E-Verify mandatory for all employers and lighten the work load on our border patrol agents, they can then put their time and resources into stopping the more serious problems pointed out earlier, criminals who run drugs, young girls as sex slaves, and terrorists who could potentially enter the country as well as deny job resources for those apparently already here.

What could be a more effective and simple answer to begin solving the border problem than to require by law that all employers use E-Verify and Americans and legal immigrants get the jobs, illegal aliens already here begin going home and others stop coming since the incentive has been removed?

Reversing the damage already done by both the current as well as past administrations actions, some by ignoring the problems and this administration through Executive Orders that are contrary to our existing laws that violates both our laws and our sovereignty could be accomplished and soon.

Remember that an "Executive Order" can be rescinded by any elected President who takes office after this administration leaves office.

Are vetted immigrants who are determined to be an asset to a country, immigrants who are judged to be people who will respect the nations values and principals, immigrants who will by their presence add to the countries economic well being and not come in and live off of the labors of others be a good thing, of course they would.

Are illegal immigrants who covertly sneak into a country an asset to the country, people who obviously do not respect the countries values laws and principals, who are not self sufficient, who apply for taxpayer services upon arrival a good thing, of course not.

Are those who come into our country on visas and then refuse to leave, those who apparently come with the intent to violate their visas and overstay any better than the border runners; the answer is obvious right?

While the U.S. has a waiting line of immigrants who want to come into the country lawfully many of our politicians seem to favor the other method, illegal immigration.

Legal immigration if conducted responsibly, allowing in an established number of people who are judged to be an effective number that would not become serious competition with legal residents for jobs or being brought in under H1, B visas as replacements for American workers and other legal immigrants currently already employed by a business merely looking to gain cheaper labor would be a good thing.

There is an important but seemingly over looked aspect on the subject of border control that is being left out of the discussion, and that is the northern border.

Americans today are concerned about the unacceptable situation that has developed on the southern U.S. border and rightly so.

However, they fail to realize that any action taken to secure the southern border will inevitably also effect the northern U.S. border as well.

If and when security on the southern border with Mexico is taken seriously and that border is made secure the northern border will become a target for criminal activity more-so than it is at present.

The proposed E-Verify virtual wall set in place by law and followed by border walls/fences in locations where they are determined to be needed would get any border solution underway much sooner than an early construction program.

Die-hard criminals will begin researching methods of replacing their lost entry points into the U.S. by way of the northern border.

However the problem for Americans goes far beyond our borders; it is a world wide problem for American citizens and legal immigrants.

Therefore any solution; any attempt at border security will have to include both the southern and the northern borders and ending the practice of people from all over the world coming to the country to give birth to make their offspring De-facto Americans.

Doing some research on the articles in the LA Times on the subject of the lucrative international anchor baby business will be a definite eye opener.

After their offspring is born in America they return home to wait until it's time to send them back as Americans.

In all reality, is the above practice any more legitimate than other methods of deceit; isn't this just another method of illegal immigration, international generational illegal immigration?

Don't just deny the facts without discovering the truth for yourself that the fourteenth amendment was set in place to prevent anyone from denying citizenship to freed slaves after the civil war.

Doing your due diligence by researching the origin of the law and its purpose will be an eye opener, you will come to know that today's birthright citizenship is a farce; an aberrational outgrowth sanctioned by the courts refusal to hear fourteen amendment cases.

What was intended to be a just law to prevent any future denial of their American citizenship and rights to freed slaves has been turned into something far beyond the intent of the author of the amendment.

If a job, any job, is worth doing it's worth doing right, a job well done would be one that while you are at it guard against all future contingencies that could come back to haunt you, past present and future.

The Supreme Court has never ruled directly on the fourteenth amendment, but the following are past comments from past Court Justices on the fourteenth amendment.

"(N)o one can fail to be impressed with the one pervading purpose found in (the 13th, 14th and 15th Amendments), lying at the foundation of each, and without which none of them would have been even suggested; we mean the freedom of the slave race, the security and firm establishment of that freedom, and the protection of the newly-made freeman and citizen from the oppressions of those who had formerly exercised unlimited dominion over him." Supreme Court opinion in the Slaughterhouse cases (1873)

"[The 14th Amendment was] primarily designed to give freedom to persons of the African race, prevent their future enslavement, make them citizens, prevent discriminating State legislation against their rights as freemen, and secure to them the ballot." Supreme Court opinion in Ex Parte Virginia (1879)

"The 14th Amendment was framed and adopted ... to assure to the colored race the enjoyment of all the civil rights that, under the law, are enjoyed by white persons, and to give to that race the protection of the general government in that enjoyment whenever it should be denied by the States." Supreme Court opinion in Strauder v. West Virginia (1880)

"The right secured to the colored man under the 14th Amendment and the civil rights laws is that he shall not be discriminated against solely on account of his race or color." Supreme Court opinion in Neal v. Delaware (1880)

"The main object of the opening sentence of the 14ᵗʰ Amendment was ... to put it beyond doubt that all persons, white or black, and whether formerly slaves or not, born or naturalized in the United States, and owing no allegiance to any alien power, should be citizens of the United States ... The evident meaning of (the words, "and subject to the jurisdiction thereof") is, not merely subject in some respect or degree to the jurisdiction of the United States, but completely subject to their political jurisdiction, and owing them direct and immediate allegiance. ... Persons not thus subject to the jurisdiction of the United States at the time of birth cannot become so afterward, except by being naturalized ..." Supreme Court opinion in Elk v. Wilkins (1884)

So by the evidence incorporated in these past statements by Supreme Court Justices they already know the intent of and the proper meaning of the wording of the 14nth amendment.

Therefore they understand full well that the present interpretation allowing the anchor baby scheme to continue is outside of law; this says it all as far as any real or even a semblence of justice is concerned in America today for American citizens.

Remember the clarafication at the time by Senator Howard "Indians born within the limits of the United States and who maintain their tribal relations, are not, in the sense of this amendment, born subject to the jurisdiction of the United States."

It wasn't until 1924 that Native American Indians were included in the 14nth amendment by legislation, which is authorized in the amendment; so the 14nth amendment can lawfully be changed by legislation and has been by wording in its text.

Logic dictates that illegal immigrants in defiance of the jurisdiction of the United States and citizens of foreign powers are not subject to the jurisdiction of the United States as required by the 14ᵗʰ Amendment.

The Supreme Court has never contridicted the above to be true so the congress with its power in the text; look it up, over immigration along with the power to enforce the Citizenship Clause can restore the correct birthright citizenship policy through legislation.

If we are to have an immigration policy that serves American citizens and legal immigrants and preserves our sovereingty it is imperative that Congress return the 14nth amendment to its original meaning.

Do some research on the practice of paying big money to have a birth registered in the U.S. the LA Times is a good place to begin.

Both present and future situations that may come into play will have to be addressed now to have any long term desired meaningful affect.

On the discussion of the northern border, not only would any type of developing situation on the northern border be harmful to Americans, but harmful to Canadians as well, and could lead to the present good relations between the two countries deteriorating over time in the future.

What would be the point of securing the southern border by increasing the Border Patrol's efficiency and eliminating the hardened criminals, drug runners, slave traders, etc if over time the same or a similar situation developed to the north?

For some time now many have been advocating that The United States build an expensive wall on our southern border; a barricade of sorts.

However, every journey begins with a first step; why not begin by implementing a virtual wall by way of E-Verify, once that is in place reevaluate the situation to determine what the next step should be.

There are currently credible estimates that as high as thirty five to forty percent of those here illegally entered the country by coming in legally on a visa then staying.

Entering the country by way of illegally running the borders is only one, although the most often used method; the lions share of illegal immigration, but the visa system abusers are still a major portion of the problem.

Any method of correcting the above thirty five to forty percent portion of the illegal immigration problem will require a plan to address this along with the unsecured border.

Why start with a border wall/fence when a virtual wall to begin with could begin eliminating all methods of illegal immigration, both those who came in and stayed as well as those who crossed the borders?

Once the virtual wall is in place begin with a program of identifying particularly problem areas of the border, then selectively put fences or walls and extra security in place in these areas as the next step.

Immediately: at the same time; follow this action by implementing mandatory E-Verify laws and identify those already here, then move ahead as the situations changes developed.

This could reasonably be expected in a short period of time to stop illegal immigrants from coming in and others already here to begin going home.

With a mandatory E-Verify system in place and enforced illegal immigrants who are here from all over the world could be identified and those who are known to be criminals in their home country, anti American aliens, known terrorists that are already here etc could be dealt with accordingly.

Once this proposed system is in place it shouldn't take that long before a reevaluation could determine exactly where and how a wall/fence should be constructed to eliminate any weak areas in our border and international security at the same time.

Why begin by building a border wall/fence that would require tweaks and changes over time to get it right when some of the problem could be taken care of before hand.

Then install walls or fences that would be more affective in dealing with the remaining issues that could be more easily identified; such as isolated smuggling points, etc.

Why isn't the obvious as well as the self evident fact that a self executing system of law at the beginning would eliminate much of the problem, and so would be the better option to begin with being discussed?

Wouldn't a better system to start with be one that wouldn't need extensive guarding, or only need a minimum of policing, one that would need very little maintenance, one that could be set in place almost immediately at relatively very little expense?

Is such a wall available and already in existence that with very little effort could soon be set in place?

The answer is yes; it does exist and could be ready to use in a reasonably short period of time.

Remember that high tech companies such as Boeing, etc, have spent time resources and effort to engineer just such a proven affective system, a virtual wall, but failed; however, we already have one that is available and working.

After reading this before dismissing it try to come up with reasons that you believe that it wouldn't work, then catalog them.

Then try to think of reasons that you believe that it could be made to work and ways to structure and implement a working system.

Balancing the pros and cons involved before reaching any conclusion may just turn out to surprise you.

As you read the following proposal remember that this system would be covering not only the border areas, but would be present in the interior for all states as well.

That fact would allow the border patrol to concentrate resources and manpower on the interdiction of truly dangerous criminals like the ones listed earlier and determine exactly what kind of barrier and where it was needed to be the most affective.

With much of the incentive for running the borders removed the lone remaining problems would be the drug runners, the potential terrorists and those involved in the illicit sex slavery trade and anchor baby trade etc.

This would obviously allow for the concentration of significantly more resources and manpower already in place to interdict and prevent much; if not all of the cross border criminal activity.

A policy of strict prosecution along with mandatory sentencing guidelines for criminals who are caught during cross border incursion during a smuggling attempt would also be affective.

While mandatory E-Verify laws may not be the full answer to the cross border drug and sex slave trade it would free up valuable resources to attack those especially despicable crimes.

Government resources that are now assigned to problems such as policing immigration issues, illegal alien criminal activity inside the country, out of work Americans while illegal aliens have the job costing taxpayers unemployment payments, government services to illegal aliens who work under the table to avoid taxes while drawing welfare are some of the problems that E-Verify would be an affective tool against.

E-Verify as a mandatory nationwide law from the beginning of the border security effort would have a positive effect on the border security equation both north and south; there would be no incentive for illegal border crossings from either the north or the south by the average person.

Gaining control of America's borders and preserving sovereignty will invariably require the problem of the average person entering the country illegally to be taken seriously and the incentives removed.

As long as the jobs magnet remains there will continue to be at least some who will cross the border illegally.

So: any solution to be truly effective will have to remove that incentive for Americans citizens and legal immigrants to improve their lives and become a part of the American dream.

The big question that people are asking is "how do you deport twelve million people" and the number is probably much higher.

The answer is easy, make E-Verify a strictly enforced mandatory federal law with sufficient penalties for violations; with the employment magnet gone those already here will begin to leave while others stop coming.

How do you stop the international anchor baby scheme that is currently taking place?

Once again the answer is an easy one; Verify a birth mothers citizenship by way of E-Verify before registering the birth as American and the problem would soon end.

Mandatory E-Verify laws would be by far the most cost effective means of insuring that our immigration laws are enforced and the border is affectively secured by requiring responsibility, honesty and vigilance by all, both the government and American employers and hospitals alike.

Also E-Verify could be used as an effective tool that already exists for the prevention of voter fraud by having a person's eligibility to receive a voter registration card instantly checked upon application and the cost would be minimal since new systems would not be needed.

E-Verify could also end the current illegal practice of some to vote in multiple districts, once registered in one district an E-Verify check could be set up and used to red flag any attempt to evade the law by double or triple registering.

Why not use a system that is available and already in place and working to insure Americans that our elections are guarded and the results are that only those eligible to vote are involved?

Anyone who would object to this type of assurance that a person's eligibility to vote is valid is definitely against eliminating voter fraud for their own personal reasons.

The charge of racism that is thrown out whenever the subject of voter verification is the issue would become moot and be instantly recognized as a spurious attempt to protect illegal voting.

Another often used but dubious charge that E-Verify would infringe on the privacy rights of American citizens is a non issue when the facts are acknowledged.

The facts are that Americans are well cataloged in many already existing government and private data basis, so those who make this objection aren't thinking rationally.

To name but a few of the government as well as private agencies that have well cataloged information on all Americans are The IRS, Social Security, Medicare, Voter Registration, Postal System, States Departments of Licensing, The U.S. Census Bureau, Veterans Administration, Banking, Credit agencies, Internet based people finders, and many others.

At this point let your thought processes tell you of the many uses for a mandatory E-Verify system, anyone applying for and eligible for government services, welfare, food stamps, or a states driver's license, or any taxpayer funded program intended for citizens could be verified within seconds.

The results would be that another incentive for illegal immigrants to come to the U.S. would be eliminated and the American taxpayer would be off the hook for supporting people who should not be in the country.

A law such as the currently proposed Kate's law, a mandatory prison sentence for second time offenders, those guilty of reentry after a deportation would be needed from the start; after all, reentry after a deportation is a federal felony.

Cities and Counties and States would necessarily have to be penalized and sanctioned that defied any federal law on the subject of harboring or failing to report illegal aliens caught in their jurisdictions.

Any state continuing to provide any social service such as public assistance, Driver's License, etc; after an E-Verify check identified them as non eligible would have to pay a high enough price to abandoned the practice.

Any law enforcement officer, or department head thereof, especially elected county Sheriffs who violate their oath of office by failing to enforce their federal immigration obligations should be removed by law.

At election time everyone should vet all candidates for the office of county Sheriff, their present position as well as their past performance would need to be taken into account.

Any and all government jurisdictions must be forced by law, and the law strictly enforced by the DOJ to cooperate fully with our immigration laws and immigration authorities, or be punished by an established method, punished by a standard that would be sufficiently severe enough to force compliance.

I personally would have no problem with a law allowing a states national guard to be called in temporarily by that states governor at the request of the U.S. Border Patrol, Customs and Immigration Service, etc to aid in any unforeseen unusual or serious situations that developed on our borders in the future.

When the situation that prompted the States National Guard to be called into service is satisfactorily brought under control the expense of the operation should be billed to the federal government.

Constitutionally the responsibility for defending the states whose borders are being violated endangering its citizens is plainly the duty of the federal government; so likewise that is where the duty to pay the bill's involved lay when they become due.

The facts are; whether people agree or not are; that half measures, patches; temporary fixes and failures to address a problem in whole are only feeble cowardly attempts that in time will only return and create even more future problems.

There are three major magnets involved in the cross border violence as described by the U.S. Border Patrol on their website.

One is the prospect of jobs that brings in one part of the illegal immigrants, although this hurts Americans who are unable to find work while the illegal immigrants have the jobs that as citizens Americans are entitled to.

Two would be the cross border sales of drugs, the cross border sales of girls as pointed out by our Border Patrol on there website, and other profits from varying criminal activities.

Three is the desire to have offspring and make them American citizens by giving birth in the U.S. all three factors combined multiply the border problems and are a path to sovereignty lost for Americans.

The Fourteenth Amendment and its grossly misapplied current interpretation by many is astoundingly naïve, even though a little research on the facts destroys the anchor baby proponent's position forced on Americans by the courts, some still believe it.

The totally erroneous statement made by many that "like it or not it's the law" and then repeat the false application of the 14nth amendment's meaning over and over shows that they parroting what they have heard others say without any due diligence, without any research involved.

A visit to the archived statement of Senator Howard the author of the 14nth Amendment who crafted and passed the fourteenth

Amendment and clarified its meaning at the time of passage, the Senator responsible for its existence puts the lie to the courts decisions and the birthright citizenship interpretation thereof.

"Every person born within the limits of the United States, and subject to their jurisdiction, is by virtue of natural law and national law a citizen of the United States. This Will not of course, include persons born in the United States who are foreigners, aliens, who belong to the families of ambassadors or foreign ministers accredited to the government of the United States, but will include every other class of persons. It settles the great question of citizenship and removes all doubt as to what persons are or are not citizens of the United States. This has long been a great desideratum in the jurisprudence and legislation of this country … Senator Jacob Howard.1866.

Anyone with a normal reading comprehension can surely understand just what the Senator was saying; what he was clarifying.

He plainly eliminates in writing those who are not included, foreigners, aliens, Ambassadors and foreign ministers families.

Every other class of persons obviously takes in the people who were the necessity for, the reason for, the fourteenth amendment and the reason it was needed and ratified.

The need and reason for the resulting amendment was to make it clear to all at the time and in the future that the recently freed black slaves were not to be a second class person under the laws of any state.

With slavery abolished all former slaves were now freeman with the constitutional right to equality under the law as United States citizens.

"A foreigner in the United States has a right to the protection of the laws; but he is not a citizen in the ordinary acceptance of the word …" Senator Edward Cowan.

As far as the jurisdiction argument many use today Senator Cowen by any and all standards clarifies that as well at the same time, obviously he knew that foreigners were to be protected while in the country, but were not the same as citizen with the same coverage under the 14nth Amendment.

When the civil war ended and African Americans were no longer slaves, but free people, there rights as Americans were still being denied and needed to be protected and that fact was obviously the reason for and the intent of the 14nth Amendment and its ratification, the above Senator's statements at the time agree.

Remember that our constitution is a contract between the states and their people, and original intent is paramount in contract law, so why do the politicians and courts of today get away with extending the original intent of protecting freed slaves far beyond its obvious original intent?

Without the rule of law faithfully adhered to no nation can exist, no successful society can continue to exist.

When the rule of law no longer applies, is no longer faithfully respected by a government, the end result can only be the eventual destruction of a nation and the existence of a lesser world experience for a people.

The death of a people; or a nation can be accomplished under an Oligarchy system where all power is concentrated in the hands of a few.

A current example would be that nine people would be given the unauthorized power to dictate the fate of a nation by decree; a nation of three hundred and thirty million people, although they were never given that power by any contractual right.

When nine people can expand the written laws to incorporate tenants by decree, pulled out of thin air, where no written law exists you have an Oligarchy.

May god forgive us, may our descendents forgive us if we don't restore our constitution as our founders gave it to us; to both our posterity, and too ourselves.

Why do we live under a system of law today that is far different than the original system of law; a system where unauthorized power is assumed and longstanding established laws are ignored, or judicially changed from the bench with impunity?

The obvious short answer is that any challenge under the current system would be ignored by the courts that have set themselves up as the all powerful branch of government, no longer one of three coequal branches.

Even though there is not one word in our constitution giving them that right; that power; both the Executive and legislative braches of government have bowed to them.

One of the arguments being used at present is that the constitution can't be changed by legislation, but apparently those same people seem to believe that the constitution can be changed by the Courts reinterpretation of the constitution's plain English wording and the statements of the authors who wrote it to suit their current bosses.

So, the mantra of many is that a constitutional amendment can't be changed by elected legislators; but it can be changed by appointed unelected judges by a reinterpretation over time, and be considered valid; really?

If the 14nth Amendment can't be changed by legislation then why did the congress in the year 1924 change it by legislation to include Native American Indians?

Legislation can not be a valid method of changing our constitution unless a change is authorized in the text of the amendment, and it is in the text of the 14nth amendment.

Today's example of this method of deceit by a court would be that according to the current Supreme Court a fine can be ruled a tax, even though the legislation in question is in writing, and again; in plain English that puts the lie to the ruling.

How about this Supreme Court ruling "WASHINGTON, June 27 - The Supreme Court ruled on Monday that the police did not have a constitutional duty to protect a person from harm, even a woman who had obtained a court-issued protective order against a violent husband making an arrest mandatory for a violation …".New York Times.

This Suprme Court ruling overturned a ruling by a federal appeals court in Colorado.

"The appeals court had permitted a lawsuit … against a Colorado town, Castle Rock, for the failure of the police to respond to a woman's pleas for help after her estranged husband violated a protective order by kidnapping their three young daughters, whom he eventually killed …".New York Times.

In my personal world veiw due to this particular ruling the all powerful Supreme Court by way of this ruling has blood on its hands along with the police department in question.

Another example would be legislating from the bench, creating rules and laws on issues where no written law passed by legislators exists.

Is this the way our system is supposed to work, a law can be declared from the bench to exist, even where no legislation passed and signed into law exists?

Isn't rewriting and/or expanding legislation from the bench as deceitful as any other method of circumventing the constitution?

So, in the opinion of judges constitutional amendments can not be changed by legislation, even when such change by legislation is authorized in the text?

But they can change it by judicial activism; change by the judicial branch of government although they were never given that power by the constitution any more than the other two branches of government were?

I have no doubt that many can personally identify other rulings that have recently imposed a rule or law where no such law was written by legislators or signed by a President that would be the basis for it.

Social engineering from the bench is rampant today by judges making decrees and others enforcing the unlegislated, unauthorized law making by fiat that is going on.

When a person or a group of people are in the process of righting gross injustices from the past that have been discovered that are multi-faceted and fail to take the necessary action to reverse them one and all at the same time, in the end, they have not accomplished a victory, they have allowed an injustice to stand.

The only remedy for the current situation is for elected legislators to get a backbone, and refuse to be considered a lower subservient branch of government.

Our constitution plainly authorizes three coequal branches of government, nowhere in the constitution does it allow for one branch to become dominant.

Legislators, who fail to stand up and be counted, and become a part of the necessary correction of this situation, need to be remembered at election time and replaced with someone who will do the job.

How did we as Americans arrive at the situation that we find ourselves in today?

The three co-equal branches of our federal government have become two subservient branches dominated by one; the Judicial Branch with no constitutional basis for this.

In spite of the ninth and tenth amendments in our Bill of Rights, the states have become totally subservient to the federal government, although many of the areas dominated by the federal government today were forbidden to it by the amendments cited.

The only areas where the states are free of federal intervention and challenge, are the areas where they seem to agree with the current administration (and past administrations) that violating federal immigration law is okay.

You seem ... to consider the judges as the ultimate arbiters of all constitutional questions, a very dangerous doctrine indeed, and one which would place us under the despotism of an oligarchy ..." Thomas Jefferson.

"The Constitution has erected no such single tribunal, knowing that to whatever hands confided, with the corruptions of time and party, its members would become despots ..." Thomas Jefferson.

"It has more wisely made all the departments co-equal and co-sovereign within themselves ..." Thomas Jefferson"

"The Constitution, in keeping three departments distinct and independent, restrains the authority of the judges to judiciary organs, as it does the executive and legislative to executive and legislative organs ..." Thomas Jefferson, Letter to William Charles Jarvis, (28 September 1820).

By the evidence of today's self assumed power (Usurpation) of supremacy, over the other two branches of our government by the judiciary Jefferson was right on the warning that, in time, an Oligarchy would be the result.

As George Washington put it; "Usurpation is the manner in which free governments are destroyed."

There have been some remedies suggested for the eventuality of serious disputes that may arise between the three coequal branches of the federal government.

My personal choice among them would be to let a majority of the states by way of their legislators and signed by their governor's make any final ruling; even nullifying any federal law.

Any disputes over the justification for laws or court rulings should be settled by the federal government's creators, not the created, after all the states predate the federal government, and are the federal government's creators.

The states created the federal government and so should by reason and logic in these matters, be considered as above their creation.

The power of nullification by the states; nullification by a majority of the states would return the federal government to three coequal branches, as originally intended.

The creator by any and all reasoning should be considered above and therefore greater than the creation and so should have any final says when it involves any disputes, if not why not?

Why stand by and allow one of the three coequal branches of the states creation to assume a power not given to it by the states; its creator, and then use that usurped position to claim supremacy over all government, including its creators, the States?

Do some research and discover that Free states challenged the hideous federal runaway slave laws refusing to return slaves to bondage and prevailed, in a truly just system this would be the norm.

During the time that I have spent traveling in other countries as a foreigner there, under international law, I had the right to the protections of their laws, however as I was a person traveling with a U.S. passport means that I was still under the jurisdiction of the United States.

If I had not been in their country legally, I would have been deported back to the United States, where as a citizen the jurisdiction would have been.

As a final thought, as a senior American citizen; I realize full well that my life experience has been a far better one than I would have experienced in any other country on planet earth.

I have traveled in Mexico and in Canada; I have traveled overseas and have not been in even one country that compares with my country, The United States of America, at least so far.

By the grace of God may The United States be returned to its roots in time to save it, and may my descendants as well as others in the future experience living, in a country that I have been blessed to have spent my life in as a citizen.

At election time all Presidential and Legislative Candidates should be questioned to give their in depth positions on sovereignty, borders and security measures they intend to be faithful to for the American people.

During court appointments Judgeship candidates should be made aware that their position is to be faithful to the constitution as written, and not to inject themselves into the legislative or executive branches domains.

Vetted legal immigrants who respect our laws yes, illegal immigrants who violate our borders and our sovereignty and once here, ignore our laws as well as disrespect our citizens, our laws and our rights to say who may come in to the country, not no but hell no.

When a government ignores its own laws that are there to protect the nation's sovereignty and its people, it is outside of the law and that means it is operating as an outlaw, right?

Outlaw defined: disobedient to or defiant of law, contemporary examples; Civic culture, meanwhile, takes less and less offense at the *outlaw* behavior of governments; synonyms, public enemy, pariah, bandit, and brigand.

This definition takes in all who defy established law, from the federal to the states, to counties and cities, to local councils and law enforcement, state police, city police and especially elected County Sheriffs; all involved that practice sanctuary policies are aiding and abetting law breakers; pure and simple.

Especially elected county Sheriffs should only be those who stand firm for the law and uphold the laws.

Since they work for and are responsible to those who elected them to their office to keep public safety as their first priority, by allowing local unlawful sanctuary city/county/state rules to go unchallenged, they are themselves operating outside of the law they took an oath to faithfully uphold.

There are far too many in government today who are professional politicians that look out for themselves instead of the people who put them in office.

This includes politicians from the local/state/federal level and politicized law enforcement at the local level who agree with sanctuary policies and act accordingly therefore they are guilty themselves of being law breakers.

It is surprising just how many people don't realize that many of the rules and regulations in their local communities that they do not agree with or are adamantly opposed to are the doings of people in their county and city commissioners' office.

All government and many of their bureaucratic rules begin at the local level, so, vet them, identify them, and vote them out for yourself and your community's sake.

Why not make "hope and change" a reality and clean up Washington D.C. your own state city and county by rejecting the current practice of reelecting the same self serving professional politicians?

Why not "Fundamentally Transform" America into a sovereign nation with secure borders for the American people once again?

This map of official sanctuary cities and counties in the U. S. does not take in the others that are covertly practicing sanctuary policies or the states that are doing the same. http://cis.org/Sanctuary-Cities-Map

Birthright citizenship facts. http://www.nationalreview.com/
birthright-citizenship-not-mandaed-by-constitution   http://
www.14thamendment.us/birthright citizenship/original intent.
html

The true history of Santa Anna and the American southwest. http://
www.andrews.edu~rwright/Oldwww/Alamo/revolution.html

Want some facts, here they are. http://www.familysecuritymatters.
org/publications/detail/trump-is-right-illegal-alien-crime-is-
staggering-in-scope-and-savagery

More facts. http://www.judicialwatch.org/blog/2015/10/sanctuary-
cities-ignore-ice-orders-to-free-9295-alien-criminals/

There are many other informative sites online if one takes the time to
do their research, remember that knowledge is power.

By: Edger J Burton … American citizen.

Foreword

My goal in writing this book is to encourage as many Americans as possible to begin doing their research on the events taking place today and the dangers that exist for our country, not only for us but more importantly for our descendants.

Our world as it exists today is a world of danger and peril: however, if we will become aware by educating ourselves as to the reasons why we are where we are we can change the world for our children and grandchildren into a better place.

The founding fathers of the United States of America, men of great courage who sacrificed both blood and treasure to pass a better world on to us where the freedoms of the individual were absolute were brave men who still hold a place of honor in our history books today.

The constitution of the United States established a country where rights were guaranteed to all Americans; our constitution still exists today, so let us return to its original principals for the sake of tomorrow's unborn child.

Through research we gain knowledge, opinions and conclusions based on a lack of the facts; not based on reality only lead to our being led down the wrong path, thus making our own future and the world a demeaned place for posterity, for our descendants, our children and grandchildren.

Only through understanding that our current system where public servants have been replaced by overlords, overlords and their financiers who have taken us down a demeaning and dangerous path can we secure a better world for others to come in the future.

Printed in the United States
By Bookmasters